Coping with Grief

My Personal Journey of Learning to Overcome Sorrow

9/25/22

ANDERSON —
YOU ARE A SPECIAL
AND WONDERFUL PERSON.
THE WORLD IS BETTER
WITH YOU IN IT.
BE WELL —
RAY

Ray Matlock Smythe

Preface

We all will suffer unbearable grief during our lifetimes. I had this experience recently with the death of my partner, Steve, with whom I shared forty-nine wonderful years. I learned how debilitating grief can be; I was and am still suffering from its effects. I learned that I had to find a way to diminish the anguish to lessen my sadness.

Over the past 20 years, I have written columns for the local paper, sharing my ideas for living a more abundant life. I enjoy using quotes from notable and ordinary people alike in my columns, some of which speak to managing grief. My friend Graham said, "Why don't you use the quotes you've collected to help yourself?" So, I took his advice and looked to some of the quotes for support.

I have used powerful quotes in this book that I believe will help people cope with their grief. I am expecting that many of the quotes will resonate with the readers of this book.

The purpose of this book is to give people some ideas, strategies, and tips on how to handle the grieving process. My hope is that these suggestions will bring people more serenity and comfort during this time of transition in their lives.

Acknowledgements

I would like to thank Elaine and Monte Johnston for all their help during Steve's illness. They were invaluable after his death to guide me through some of the financial matters and legal papers. Both Elaine and Monte gave me emotional support and lots of hand holding during this tough time in my life.

A huge thanks to Graham Hookey for helping me put this book together, and for giving me the idea of using quotations to help me and others deal with their grief. I also want to thank Graham for the photo that graces the cover of the book. It is Champney's Cove in Newfoundland.

I would like to thank Sid Pearce for making this book come to life with his excellent computer skills and editing assistance. His help was invaluable in getting this book published.

Thanks to all our many friends and relatives who sent cards, brought food, delivered flowers, and gave me emotional support. Your thoughtfulness was overwhelming.

Dedication

I dedicate this book to Steve Edward Oliver. He was my partner, soulmate, and rock for 49 years. Steve taught me so many lessons about living. I do and will miss him deeply the rest of my life.

I have included his obituary at the end of the book.

I lost my partner, Steve Edward Oliver, in February of 2022. We had been together since 1973. We were both turning 73 in 2022. We had almost been together for a half a century.

Steve had been an outstanding chiropractic physician in our home city of Portland, Oregon. He was named the Chiropractor of the Year for the whole state when he was only twenty-nine. His first patient was my dad.

Besides having a private practice, Steve was also the Dean of Western States Chiropractic College which is now called the University of Western States. After years in that position, he went back to the clinic to teach students chiropractic techniques. He loved working with the students.

We decided to move to Palm Springs, California in 2001. We wanted to start a new life in warm weather and a smaller town. Steve opened his practice, but he only practiced for several years when he came down with Lupus.

The tragedy of his life was having to retire early. He bravely fought Lupus for 22 years. When he went to the hospital, I thought he would rally, get better and return home. It never happened. He just stopped breathing early one night. I wasn't prepared for that to happen.

I can't adequately express the pain, sorrow, and loss I felt. It was beyond heartbreaking. I wrote a column about grief for the local newspaper. I had more responses from that column than any other column I had written in twenty years. Several people suggested I write a book about grief, sorrow, loss, and recovery. So that is how this book got started. It is a book on how to cope with the loss of a loved one. It is full of ideas and strategies to help people deal with their grief.

Everyone grieves differently and on their own time schedule. My hope and expectation is that some of these ideas and thoughts will help give the reader some comfort to navigate through the grieving process.

"The irony of grief is that the person you need to talk to about how you feel is the person that is no longer there."

Unknown

This quote from an unknown author really nails how many people feel. Those readers who have lost someone special know its power and truth.

Steve and I were excellent communicators. We talked about everything. Our favorite place to converse was our casual dining room table that looked out to our small swimming pool. It was the perfect setting for discussing politics, life, or problems. Our dogs would always sit under the table hoping for a scrap after one of our discussions.

Now I am sitting there alone and missing those conversations immensely.

I have solved this problem by calling friends and talking to them about a particular issue or challenge. I think therapists are great, but I believe your peers can offer some great and free advice. I think using the phone and talking to someone is the best way.

Yes, I do text people early in the mornings, but I still feel that hearing a human voice is better than a text if you really want a long discussion.

I also invite people over for coffee or drinks on a regular basis. We sit at the same dining room table that Steve and I sat at all of those many years. Having people over is easy if you don't have to cook a meal. I always provide some appetizers which usually are chips and dips. Occasionally, I might buy something at Trader Joe's and cook it in the oven. My point is that you can have people to talk to about your grief situation if you just pick up the phone and invite them over. The benefits of talk therapy with people you love, and trust are immeasurable.

No one will ever replace your loved one that you talked to for years, but having other adults over is a huge step in helping yourself feel better.

"Be careful about the shoulds in your life or you will should all over yourself."

Betty Thomasson

This funny quote is right on. It was told to me by my therapist friend, Betty. She was right.

Many people including myself, go down that rabbit hole of saying, "I should have said this, or I should have done that." Don't go there.

We are all humans with flaws and blemishes. Sure, there were things I think I might have done differently when Steve was in the hospital. I can list a few, but I did the best I could. I am not a medical person.

I would spend three hours in the mornings with him and then drive home for lunch and let the dogs outside. Then I would go back and spend three hours in the afternoon. I would usually leave at three. Driving back and forth to the hospital was exhausting. Being in the hospital with Steve was tiring. He didn't feel like talking much and there were so many interruptions. Technicians doing tests on him, nurses giving him IV's and doctors coming in to assess the situation.

Sometimes I thought I "should" have stayed longer, but Steve was in and out of sleep. One of my friends said it best when he reminded me about the last time I was ill . . . did I really want to talk or even relish having someone around? Well, the answer could be a yes or a no. I realized that Steve was in his own world and although he was glad I was there, I felt invisible at times.

One doctor toward the end took me out in the hall. He put his hand on my shoulder and said, "I absolve you of any guilt. You can get caregivers syndrome which tires you out so much you get sick. You must take care of yourself first."

He was right. I was getting physically and emotionally exhausted. I had to take care of myself, the house and our two dogs. None of us have any training for these life and death events. We do the best we can to be helpful to our loved ones.

The point is to not get trapped in the "shoulds." It will simply wear you down and make you depressed. Remember that you did the best you could at a time of great distress.

"Prepare in advance for the Inevitable."

No one ever expects to die. We all try to pretend it will never happen to us. It will always happen to another wife, husband, brother, sister, or friend. We like to be in denial.

It is especially important to make a will or trust.

If you make a trust, you won't have to have it probated. A will can be taken to court, but it all depends on your family and how they react to the conditions of the will. Where money is concerned, people can get crazy with greed.

Be sure to spell out who gets what in your trust/will. Steve wanted to give his niece and four nephews a small amount of money. He wrote this in the trust. Since I was the executor, I wrote out five checks. They were thrilled to get a few extra dollars in their bank accounts. The rest of his estate went to me. We had planned that from the beginning that we would both give each other our estates.

The second most important thing is cremation or funeral arrangements. We decided to be cremated and hired a cremation company. We agreed to pay it off quickly so it would not be an issue when either of us died.

It turned out that the cremation company had changed their benefits. One substantial change was that they no longer provided death certificates. This was a huge inconvenience, as the death certificate form the cremation company gave me to complete was incorrect. After weeks of frustration, I had to drive to Riverside which was an hour away to get the death certificates and pay additional fees that were not specified on the form. Death certificates are extremely important. You need them for many financial and legal matters. My advice is to periodically check with your cremation company or funeral home to see if there have been any major changes in their policies since you purchased your contract with them.

Social Security is another big task. Often your Social Security check will change. You need to call them and then present your marriage license and a death certificate to receive any new benefits. They will not accept photocopies so have a certified copy.

Share with your spouse your passwords for all your phones, computers, iPads, and other technical devices. Also, know the pin numbers for your checking and savings accounts as well as any other financial investments.

Closing phone accounts and credit cards takes time. Go at your own speed. It doesn't all have to be done at once. You are going to deal with lots of paperwork, but you will also be dealing with daily grief. It is imperative that you pace yourself.

"Stay Engaged with Others."

It is most important to stay connected with family and friends during this time of transition.

We were blessed with many friends. They were all saints after Steve died. They brought over food, flowers, liquor, and love. I appreciated their kindness so much.

It is important to accept invitations for dinners, lunches, drinks, or a cup of coffee. You may not feel like it for a short time, but it is emotionally healthy to get out of the house. Say yes, to those phone calls or text messages asking you out.

You can also be the catalyst for asking your friends and family over to your home. You don't have to cook a huge dinner. Just either have them over for drinks and appetizers or coffee and cookies. People love to be invited and your peers can help you with good advice and comfort during this unsettling time in your life.

We can always learn from someone else. I have learned so much about how to handle grief from my friends and family. Of course, you may not agree with some people's advice about sorrow. Just accept the pieces of wisdom that work for you.

I have said it before and it is so true, we all grieve differently. Having said that, I have found that staying engaged with others has helped me immensely on so many levels.

"Little by little, grief slowly fades. But love always burns brightly."

Unknown

I think this is a helpful quote. We grieve the loss of our special someone, but the tears eventually begin to fade. We need to concentrate on the love we had with that special individual.

It is not healthy to keep thinking about the actual illness, the medical crises, the time in the nursing home or the hospital stays. These are simply downers. Sure, we all can wake up in the middle of the night and visualize those unhappy times. Again, it is not emotionally healthy to do so.

The mind is amazing. You have control of your thoughts. Once you start thinking of all the love you had with your special person, the grief is easier to deal with daily. Remember the fun times, the special birthdays or parties or the vacations. Concentrate on visualizing those kinds of events and the love will burn brightly.

Dale Carnegie said it best, "Feeling sorry for yourself and your present condition, is not only a waste of energy, but the worst habit you could possibly have."

Yes, he is brutally honest, but Dale is right. My partner told me to mourn his death for a brief time and then live life to the fullest. His advice was just like Mr. Carnegie's wisdom. Continue to visualize the good times and love will continue to burn brightly in your memories.

"Death ends a life, not a relationship."

Mitch Albom

I love this quote. I think it is such a wonderful and perceptive way to deal with the loss of a loved one.

One woman told me that she continued to work after her husband had passed. Each night when she drove home, she would talk to her husband about her day. The good parts and the challenging ones. She said that she didn't know if he could hear her or not, but it made her feel better.

Several people shared that they journaled their thoughts to their special person. Some did it on the computer while others hand wrote messages in a three ringed notebook.

Others put their arms around the urn holding the ashes of their spouse, relative or friend and spoke to them. My housekeeper still does this when she comes to the house. She talks to Steve for a few minutes and then starts working on the house.

All the above acts are demonstrating that the life may be gone, but the relationship never left. Folks need to do what makes them feel good and gives them comfort. There is no right or wrong when it comes to grief.

My friend Betty who was a wonderful therapist once said, "You know what is best for you." I think those are truly wise words.

"Stay Physically Active."

It is imperative that you have some physical activity. Sitting all day is not good for any of us. We spend too much time sitting at our computers and dining room tables. I read recently that you should get up every 20 minutes if you are typing at your computer and walk around the house or outside.

I live in the Palm Springs desert community. It is easy to get up and take a morning walk. I know for some other parts of the country that might be more challenging. You could always go to a mall or a gym if the weather is too bad outside.

The importance of physical activity is that it makes you feel better mentally. After the death of a spouse, friend or relative, you need to help your mental health with activity.

I walk every day and it really helps my mood. It is difficult to be depressed when you see the beauty of the mountains, flowers, and sunshine.

Find a person or persons to walk with you every day. Walking with others makes you walk every day. If you walk alone, you can always find an excuse to not walk. So, it is better to walk with a group or a friend. They won't let you take a walking vacation.

"Have One on One Conversations with Others Who Have Lost Their Loved One."

I was not prepared for Steve to die. After his death, I didn't know which way to turn. I needed help. So, I decided I would ask friends who had lost their spouses to come to the house for drinks or coffee.

This was a great idea. I learned so much from my fellow peers about grief, loss, and sorrow. I interviewed eight friends.

One thing they all said was that time does not totally heal the grief. It just makes it more comfortable and easier to handle. Time helps to push out the sad memories and bring the happy ones back into your mind. So, the old expression of "time heals everything" was shattered by these conversations with my friends.

Another news flash for me was that all the couples did not have perfect relationships. They had arguments and times where they did not get along. This was a relief for me as we had our ups and downs and I wondered if we were the only ones. Guess what? We were like most couples with highs and lows.

As my friend Kevin said, "You were human. You had your flaws and failings. Everyone does. So don't beat yourself up." I recommend one on one conversations as they really are helpful and instructional.

"You Are Not on a Time Schedule."

One of the mistakes I made was thinking I had to do everything all at once. I had to call Social Security, Verizon, Visa, and other financial institutions.

Steve's brother and my brother are both named David. Both Davids reminded me that nothing had to be done immediately. In other words, complete one task at a time.

I decided to tackle Social Security first. It was easy. I phoned them and we set up an appointment for an agent to interview me. They ask a lot of questions, but you know the answers to them. The only thing I had to do was bring our marriage license to the Social Security office.

The more difficult tasks were dealing with his IRA's. Even though I was the beneficiary, there was a large amount of paperwork to fill out. I had Monte/Elaine help me with those forms. Plus, I called the companies for more help. It is all written in legalize so you need assistance from others.

The most important task is to get the death certificates. I would start with at least six. You need them for closing and opening accounts.

Again, nothing must be done immediately. Steve's ashes are in an urn in the living room. He wants them spread on the Pacific Ocean. It doesn't have to be done right away.

You have been through a lot so just take a chill pill and get to your tasks when you are well enough to deal with them.

"If you are going through Hell, keep going.

Winston Churchill

Churchill was a word star. He could come up with some wonderful lines. I love this quote.

Let's face it, when your loved one dies, you go through Hell. You are dealing with the worst thing that has ever happened to you. You must keep pushing yourself forward.

We had dogs for all the years we were together. Steve and I made our own dog food. It was quite the operation. We would peel carrots and then put them in a blender. We would boil chicken breasts and then put them into the food processor. The rice cooker provided all the rice we needed. We would take all the ingredients and put them into a huge bowl. Then we would start filling Tupperware bowls to freeze. It was a big operation.

The other day I started making dog food on my own. I felt like I was going through Hell. I didn't think I could do it by myself as it was making me so darn sad. However, I pushed myself through it and got it done.

My Mom used to say, "This too shall pass." She was right. You do get through it, but it is tough. Keep going and you will get through whatever task or feeling upsets you.

"Grief is the price we pay for love."

Queen Elizabeth II

I believe that Queen Elizabeth really nails it with her quote.

We wouldn't grieve if we hadn't loved. It is part of the life process that we are saddened by the loss of a special person.

She has certainly seen and experienced plenty of grief in her life. The untimely death of her father, the King of England. The thousands of English citizens who died during the Nazi Blitz of London during World War II. She drove an ambulance and helped get injured people to the hospitals. Princess Di's sudden death in that horrific automobile accident. Of course, the recent death of her husband Prince Phillip.

Queen Elizabeth is a role model for dealing with grief. She pushed through them all and kept moving forward. I know she must have her moments, but she has a strong spirit that exudes resilience. Queen Elizabeth teaches us that life goes on whether we want it to or not.

"Don't cry because it is over. Smile because it happened."

Dr. Seuss

This is one of my favorite quotes. It applies to our discussion about sorrow, loss, and grief. It is such a simple concept.

Yes, we are going to cry and feel that tight spot in our stomachs over the death of our loved one. However, if you push yourself, you can turn that slowly around.

Smiling about all the wonderful times you had with each other. Steve and I traveled the world when we were younger. We went to Europe, China, Hong Kong, Hawaii, Mexico, the Caribbean, Greece, cruises to Alaska and even wonderful National Parks like Yellowstone. I see those pictures on our walls and they make me smile. I don't get sad but am so happy we had the opportunity to enjoy such places.

I see the pictures of our dogs on the walls of our home. They brought us such joy. I don't cry but smile because of all the years of unconditional love they gave us. So, if you can twist your thinking around a bit, use Dr. Seuss's quote to help you feel better during this time of challenge.

"There are no good-byes for us. Wherever you are, you will always be in my heart."

Gandhi

This is such a soothing thought. I often look up to the blue sky and think that Steve is up there looking down on me. We always talked about the idea of energy. Energy never dies so we felt that the energy of the soul must survive after death. Who knows for sure, but it is a reassuring thought.

Everyone has different ideas about what happens after you die. Some folks are deeply religious while other people are agnostic or atheists. Some people believe in Heaven and others believe the only Hell is here on Earth. Each person has their own beliefs that give them strength and courage during this rough time of loss.

Gandhi's thought gives me comfort as it simply means your loved one is always with you. Whether you are in the middle of an ocean or out in the desert, your special person will always be with you. I think it is a soothing concept.

"There are worse things than death."

Steve Oliver

This might be a bit controversial for some people depending on the cause or circumstances of the death of their loved one.

Steve had been sick with Lupus for over 22 years. He was in terrible pain, on oxygen 24/7 and had many other medical problems. During the last few years of his life, he would go to bed and tell me he was ready to go. Steve would say he was staying alive only for me and the dogs.

I understand where he was coming from saying those words. He had been suffering from so many major ailments through the years and his poor body just wasn't responding to new treatments.

He wasn't afraid of death and didn't feel like it was something to obsess about either. He just believed death would put him out of his constant pain and discomfort. His life had become isolated only leaving the house for doctor appointments or going to the neighbors.

One of my issues was feeling so bad that he died before he expected to but knowing how he felt, I get it. It still makes me terribly sad, but if it brought him peace, then I accept it.

"Activity and Sadness are Incompatible."

Unknown

This quote is like a stick of dynamite. It is so clear and powerful.

Busy people are happy people. Sitting around feeling sorry for yourself just doesn't cut it. Your loved one would not want you mourning forever. Betty White said, "Keep busy with your work and your life. You can't become a professional mourner." She was right.

Betty White lost her husband many years ago, but she kept on working and living. She got involved in the Los Angeles Zoo project and helped countless animals. She continued with her television sitcoms and became even more successful and famous as she got older.

Rose Kennedy told all her children that "Service to others and the community brings you happiness." She was correct. Get out and get busy with volunteer organizations that turn you on. Don't volunteer or go to work for some company for which you don't feel passion. Passion for a cause or an issue will make you feel alive again.

Check out your newspaper or Google volunteer positions in your city. You will find it rewarding and a great distraction from your grief.

"The greatest healing therapy is friendship and love."

Hubert H. Humphrey

Many people I talked to reached out to family and friends after their special person died. It seemed that the need for human companionship was paramount at this time.

Time and time again, people needed the solace of family and friends to help them through this ordeal of sadness.

Some folks do isolate. Like I have said before, everyone grieves differently and there is no correct way.

I might add here that some of your friends simply don't know what to say or do. They may stay away from you. Some friends are better phoning you or others just sending you a card or flowers. Others may bring you food. People do what they are comfortable doing.

Having said that, some of your friends may do nothing. They may be at a loss of knowing what to do. I don't think you should obsess about this at all. Let it go. Take care of yourself first.

Quite frankly, I was shocked at how sweet many people were to me when Steve died. People I didn't know well, sent cards with lovely notes inside. Your friendships with others will give you love that will help you heal. Welcome it.

"Love is the great miracle cure. Loving ourselves works miracles in our lives."

Louise Hay

During this sad time in your life, you need to love yourself more. Yes, we can be so critical of ourselves at times like these.

Human beings are funny. They constantly pick out the negative parts of their bodies, personalities, or life experiences. Right now, forget about all of those.

Love yourself so you can love others during this challenging time. If you love yourself, you can give comfort and love to those who need it. Death doesn't just affect one person. It is like the pebble thrown into the pond which creates little waves across the water. Losing someone affects many people. Reaching out to others with a warm hug, a smile, or a kind word is what is needed now so desperately.

Stop the negative talk about yourself and love the wonderful you.

"You are a gift to the universe, believe it always." Unknown

"Your heaviest artillery will be your will to live. Keep that big gun going."

Norman Cousins

I must admit that after Steve died, I didn't care if I lived any longer. There was such an emptiness in my soul that it just seemed pointless to live without him. He and I had been together since we were 23 years old. We had shared 49 years of history. We knew the same people, had the same educational experiences, knew both our families so well and had all those wonderful trips. What was the purpose of life now? What was the point of living without him?

I am sure others have had the same thoughts. Of course, I had to snap out of it. One way I did this was because Steve told me to live a full life after he was gone. He told me that he would die first, and he wanted me to thrive after his passing not just survive.

My first step to thriving was to write this book. It has been most therapeutic, and I believe it will be helpful to others.

So, I continue to push myself to stay involved in the Osher Lifelong Learning Institute here in the desert and continue to do my writing. Plus, I still have a highly active social life as I really do enjoy people. So, keep that big gun going like Mr. Cousins's suggested.

"Always keep your sense of humor. You will need it more and more as you age."

Elizabeth Smythe

How can we talk about humor when we are talking about something so serious as death? Well, it is quite logical. We cannot be in a constant state of grief. Humor and laughter make a person healthier.

My Mom was a great role model for her quote. She lost her youngest son when he was only thirty-nine. We had a very small funeral for my brother Danny. However, we had a large celebration of life party for him after the funeral. It was great to be with friends of all different ages. There was both laughter and tears.

Mother had many more challenges in her life, but she always kept her sense of humor. It is not being disrespectful to your loved one who has passed. It is about taking care of yourself.

As the years passed, she had a hip replacement and a knee replacement. She always said she went to the doctor for "maintenance work" like an old car. When she would forget something, she would call it a Senior Moment. She died at 79 of cancer. Her wonderful spirit and laughter gathered her many friends through the years. The church overflowed at her funeral. People came to pay their respects to someone who loved to laugh and would try to find humor in even the most trying situations. Keep your sense of humor!

> **"I am a strong person, but every now and then I also need someone to take my hand and tell me everything will be alright."**
>
> Unknown

This quote is touching. Everyone feels like this especially after the passing of a special person in their life.

This is the time not to be embarrassed to pick up the phone and call someone. Trust me, I have called up friends and told them I was having a bad afternoon. Could I come over for drink? The answer has always been a yes. People understand that grief ebbs and flows.

Recently, I was having a rough day. I had been listening to music and doing some correspondence at my desk. I was also paying Steve's bills. I started getting sad and a little weepy. The phone rang and friends of mine asked if I would like to come over for dinner. My first reaction was to say no as I was so down. However, I realized that I figuratively needed someone to hold my hand so I said I would love to come to supper.

It turned out to be just what I needed. I felt so much better for spending the evening with friends.

My advice is to not be shy about asking for help and don't turn down invitations just because you are not feeling 100%.

"Nobody can give you wiser advice than yourself."

Marcus Tullius Cicero

After a person dies, you are flooded with advice on how to deal with everything.

I remember one of the first things people said to me was, "Are you going to sell one of the cars?" Well, that was about the last thing I was thinking about! I was more concerned how I was going to get through the next hour or day without Steve by my side.

Another person wanted to know if I was going to sell the house. A friend asked if I was going to take a long vacation? I had to let these questions go by the wayside.

My therapist friend, Betty said, "Ray knows what is best for Ray." Those are true words. Trust your own judgment and go with your intuition during this time of sadness and transition.

Of course, you can have discussions with your friends and family about homes, cars, vacations, pets, finances, etc. However, when push comes to shove, go with your feelings. Let your heart direct you.

You know what is best for you. Don't be pushed into hasty decisions.

"It is not the strongest of the species that survives, nor the most intelligent that survives. It is the one that is most adaptable to change."

Charles Darwin

Death means change in your life. It means major changes in your world as you had known it before your special person passed.

You must adapt to a new world without your loved one. Let's face it, it is darn tough. We are creatures of habit and the older you are the harder it is to adapt to change.

Steve and I always had coffee and read the morning paper together each morning for almost 49 years. The dogs would sit under the table sleeping but were always hoping for a morning treat.

My new normal is making my own coffee and reading the paper by myself. No more discussing the articles with him. The dogs are still here, but it isn't the same. I have had to adapt to the fact that he won't be there with me. I don't like it at all. As a matter of fact, I hate it. However, I know I can't change it, so I have to accept it or be depressed the rest of my life.

Everything has changed now. I no longer discuss what we are going to have for dinner, who we want to play cards with or do we want to get new front doors. It is all up to me now. I can do it even though it is not fun by yourself. It is my new normal and I must adapt. So will you.

"Life will bring you pain all by itself. Your responsibility is to create joy."

Milton Erickson

Rose Kennedy was a true role model for courage and grace after the deaths of her sons and daughter. She said it was her faith that kept her strong. Having said that, Rose said it was also helping others that also made life worth living. She maintained an active role in several charities throughout her home state and in the country. Mrs. Kennedy created joy for others on many levels.

We need to do the same thing on any level we choose. Of course, we are sad, darn sad. However, we can't just sit in the house or office each day being depressed or mad. We need to make a difference.

One of my friends was recently divorced. He equated it like a death as he is alone now. He decided to volunteer at a local elementary school. He is a buddy to the kids and a reader to them as well. He only does it once or twice a week, but he loves it.

Another friend of mine is a retired teacher. She lost her spouse several years ago. She spends her time planning reunions with her grade school and high school friends. These reunions take a lot of work, but they bring immense joy to people who attend them.

When you are emotionally ready, find ways to bring joy to others. It will bring happiness to you as well.

"Life has two rules: Number 1, never quit. Number 2, always remember rule number 1."

Duke Ellington

Yes, it would be easy to quit. It would be simple to shut the door and isolate. It would be effortless to stay in bed all day.

Would that make you happy or content? I doubt it very much. You must put on your big boy or big girl pants and face the world. You still have lots to live for and offer the world. One of my favorite quotes is: "You are a gift to the universe, believe it always."

One activity you could consider is taking up some old hobbies that you have left behind for years. Many people are not ready for volunteer work or a job after the death of a loved one. However, you can re-start that hobby of yours.

My Dad is a wonderful piano player. He had me take piano lessons for years, but I haven't played the piano in ages. It sits in the living room gathering dust. I was thinking about starting to play again and even taking lessons.

How about your hobbies? Are you a crafts person? Do you sew? Do you paint or play an instrument? Perhaps starting off with one of your forgotten avocations is an effective way to get back into the swing of life.

The bottom line is to remember that you are not allowed to quit.

"In three words I can sum up everything I've learned about life…it goes on."

Robert Frost

One of our greatest poets wrote those words. Robert Frost was brutally right.

When Steve died my life stopped, but not for long as life wouldn't let me stop. The dogs needed to be fed, the gardener had to be paid, one of the cars needed repair, and the phone had to be answered.

I was shocked that life went on, but how could it not? Steve was only one person among billions of people. I was only one individual who had lost his soulmate. So maybe it is a blessing that life goes on without our loved one. Maybe it is the universe trying to keep the world spinning.

I still had to pay the mortgage, buy groceries, call family members, and get death certificates. Life just did a 180 degree turn. I just kept going and didn't look back. I tried to keep up with all the bills and responsibilities of running a household. It is not easy when you are used to having another person helping you for almost 49 years.

I am learning how to do it, but I still don't have it down to perfection. It just will take time and soon I will settle into a new routine. Life goes on and hopefully, it will get better for everyone who has lost their special person.

"Life does not have to be perfect to be wonderful."

Annette Funicello

This book talks about grief, but also about moving on with your life.

Life has never been perfect for anyone. Brave Annette Funicello died from multiple sclerosis. She was in chronic neuropathic pain. She always had a positive attitude and never complained.

Annette reminded me of small children who have cancer but can still find joy in their daily lives. If these young children with cancer can find happiness, then we can do the same as adults.

I am reminded of my mother who raised four teenage boys and two large dogs. It was impossible to keep the house clean especially growing up in Portland, Oregon where it was always raining. We would all come into the house with wet and muddy shoes. Plus, the dogs never were able to wipe their paws! My Mom did the best she could, but it was a losing proposition. Did she get upset?

No, she had an enthusiastic sense of humor and was not going to live her life cleaning the house. She participated in everything from community service, bridge clubs, golfing, church activities and an active potluck group. She lived life to the fullest. Was life perfect? No, but she had lots of fun and made others feel great with her sense of humor.

"So far, you've survived 100% of your worst days. This too shall pass."

Unknown

Isn't this an amazing quote? Think about all the terrible things that have happened in your life. Guess what? You are still here, and the problems are gone, or you are managing them.

I put this quote in as sometimes I feel we will never get through this grief and sadness we experience. Somedays are good, but then like the ocean waves coming to the shore, I get covered with sands of sorrow. Having said that, it eventually recedes, and I am able to cope.

Sometimes I think I have a guardian angel that protects me from awful things. Most of the time everything works out well. You always worry about the worst that could happen. Remember that 90% of what you worry about never happens. It is an amazing fact.

I think this quote is helpful to remember as you go through the very first weeks and months of your loss. When you think you can't make it, recall the quote to help you through the tough moment or situation. You can do it. You have survived before, and you will again now.

"Grief is two parts. The first is loss. The second is the remaking of life."

Anne Roiphe

We can all relate to the first sentence about loss. The loss of your loved one will last a lifetime. Each person will process their grief differently.

The second part is more challenging. How do you go about creating a new life? Do you remain in your present house? Do you move to a new city? Do you buy a new car? Do you start dating? These are just a few of the myriad of questions to be answered.

The adage is not to make any major moves or decisions until one year has gone by. I think that is still good advice. Everything is still too raw.

The most important decision for me is where to live. I have chosen to stay in our present home. Why? Well, first it is all one level with no stairs. Second, my close friends all live in this neighborhood. I have other friends, but they are only a few miles away. Moving to a different neighborhood or city would be emotional suicide for me. Plus, our neighborhood is close to everything. Most importantly, I have years of memories here in this house that make me feel good.

Everyone must make their own decisions about moving but be careful not to make a quick decision that you might regret later.

"Your struggles develop your strengths. When you go through hardships and decide not to surrender, that is strength."

Arnold Schwarzenegger

Struggling with grief is challenging. Grief doesn't play fair. It is insidious at times by catching you off guard and then piercing your heart with pain. Sometimes it is so overwhelming you think you can't go on any longer. You feel like giving up and life isn't worth living.

This is when your inner strength comes to play. You must stand up to the grief. You have to say. "I am stronger than you. You cannot strangle me. I am not going to be hostage to your controlling thoughts."

You are truly stronger than you think. You have heard that expression before, but it is true. Millions of people have gone through the grief process successfully. They did not surrender to the dark side but came out standing tall and feeling the sunshine on their faces.

I realize that grief is part of loss, but it is too easy for many of us to get stuck in the quicksand of grief. So being strong and not surrendering to it 24/7 is very healthy. Again, you must force yourself to get out of bed and face the day with a positive attitude. You can do it and will realize how strong you really are each day.

"Those we love don't go away, they walk beside us every day...unseen, unheard, but always near, still loved, still missed and very dear."

Unknown

This is a comforting thought.

 I feel this quote when I am walking in the mountains, beach, or desert. The beauty of each of these places is strikingly different, but I feel that my loved ones are out there in that universe.

Friends have shared with me that they feel their loved ones are around them when hummingbirds come to their feeders. They seem to hover around them and not necessarily go for the nectar first.

Sometimes when I am driving, I feel that Steve is in the car with me. It is hard for me to concentrate, and it always makes my heart ache. It is the strangest feeling as it is a combination of an ache and an emptiness in my chest cavity.

Again, each person can interpret this quote about grief differently. Most importantly, I just find this quote beautiful and full of serenity.

"Believe in fresh starts and new beginnings."

Unknown

I have a dear friend Joan whose husband died instantly from a heart attack. It was devastating. She loved him very much and there wasn't time to say good-bye.

She decided to go back to work where she was a successful HR person in a large organization. Joan was perfect for the job as she had experienced the ultimate sadness of losing a spouse without any warning. Everyone loved this woman as she had the knack of having compassion for others because of her own sad background. Her smile and fun personality made her an enormous success at her job.

Eventually, she retired and moved to a new state. She wanted a change of scenery and new adventures. Dating has been problematic, but she is open to it.

Dating is always a challenge. Each romance is different, and you often compare it to your first spouse. Again, try to be open to new situations. Go out for coffee and lunch. If you find there is no electricity between the two of you, perhaps it will turn into a close friendship.

Be open to new beginnings, friendships, and romances. You never know who might be around the corner to change your life.

"When you give of yourself, you never die, because you live in the hearts of everyone you've ever touched."

Mitch Albom

This is such a lovely thought.

I know that my partner Steve touched many lives. He was a chiropractor with skilled hands and intuitive intelligence. So many people wrote me after his death how he had helped them with their pain.

Folks wrote that he was the best doctor they had ever been to in their lives. Repeatedly patients would say he was the only one who could take their pain away and keep it gone. They complimented him on his professionalism and kindness.

Sometimes his patients would cry after he adjusted them as they were so overcome with emotion. What a fantastic legacy for Steve. Although he was forced to retire because of his Lupus, he would often work on friends. People still come up to me and say how Steve gave them the best adjustment of their lives.

Steve's spirit still exists as he lives in the hearts of the patients he adjusted. The same is true for your loved one. You don't need to be a doctor to touch hearts. If you feel down, read this quote often. It is so upbeat and loving.

"Sleep is the greatest healer."

Elizabeth Anderson

This quote was written by a nurse in a large hospital. Elizabeth felt that sleep was so important to a patient's health and well-being.

Sleeping well after the death of a loved one is imperative. Both your body and brain have been overtaxed with emotions and stress. Your whole body has been assaulted with feelings it has not experienced before so it is important to get your sleep.

Most doctors will tell you that sleeping in a very dark room is important. Do not watch television in bed or play on your cell phone. Keep the bedroom as your place for deep sleep. It is also helpful to keep your bedroom cool. I believe between 65 and 68 degrees is the recommended temperature.

Adults should get between eight to nine hours of sleep. Try to go to bed at the same time each night and that should help you to get into a routine that your body recognizes.

If you are like me, I wake up early in the morning around 2:30 or 3:30 a.m. Then I start thinking about my loss. This is not a good thing. So, I have to really concentrate on going back to sleep thinking about pleasant things like vacations. If I have a bad night, I will take a short nap in the afternoon.

Recent studies about the importance of sleep have proliferated in the last few years.

A lack of sleep can cause all sorts of diseases and shorten your life. You can die from a lack of sleep before dying from a lack of food. I forget the actual numbers, but it is staggering how lack of sleep can hurt your body.

Of course, it's not always easy to get a good night's sleep, but if you try some of the suggestions, I have given you, I believe you will sleep better.

Remember this quote as I believe it is so beneficial to our good health.

> **"The secret of health for both mind and body is not to mourn for the past, not to worry about the future, or not to anticipate troubles, but to live in the present moment wisely and earnestly."**
>
> Buddha

Living in the moment is basic to our emotional wellness especially during the grief period after our loved one passes.

Another way of expressing this thought is called living in the Now. The idea is to stay focused on the exact moment you're living in during the day.

I remember going out to lunch several weeks ago. My mind started to wander off to thinking about Steve in the hospital and the weeks after he died. I turned my mind off and concentrated with all my might to be in the moment. Guess what? It worked. I had a delightful lunch with friends and enjoyed the afternoon.

It takes work to focus on the present, but like anything, it can become a habit if you practice it each day. Grief tries to steal your happiness at times but living in the moment gives you a vacation from your sorrow.

"Sometimes life knocks you on your ass…get up, get up, get up!!! Happiness is not the absence of problems, it's the ability to deal with them."

Steve Maraboli

This quote is rather brutish, but it tells it like it is. When you have a death, you get knocked down emotionally. It takes a lot of strength to get back up on your feet.

Your friends and family can tell you to how to get up, but until you have the will to do so, you will stay down. Sometimes you just must take baby steps as you slowly get up to face your new world.

I remember my first principal. I was discouraged and felt overwhelmed my first year of teaching. I taught in a low-income middle school and the kids were tough. I told her that I just didn't think I could continue with all my teaching responsibilities.

She put her hand on my shoulder and said, "Do one task at a time. Finish it and then go on to the next one. You will be fine."

I would give folks who have just lost a loved one the same advice. Finish one project and then go to the next. I took the project of Social Security first after Steve's death. After I finished with that, I went on to securing the death certificates. By focusing on one project, it is easier to get up, get moving and deal with the issue at hand.

"In spite of all that doctors know, and their studies never end, the best cure of all when spirits fall, is a kind note from a friend."

John Wooden

This book has been about managing your grief through quotes after the loss of a loved one.

While I was going through the grieving process several friends of mine died. I took the time to write a sympathy card to their spouses.

Writing the notes was very cathartic for me. I certainly could understand their loss as mine was so fresh and raw. They appreciated my words and it made me feel good that I helped them a bit.

Sometimes we get so caught up in our own grief we forget that others are going through the same sorrow. It is healthy for us to think of others and give them strength during these rocky days of sadness.

Yes, e-mails count as notes. However, I believe that a handwritten note is much more meaningful. I guess that I am old school on that thought. The bottom line is do what works for you. The important thing is to write a note to your friend.

"If I were asked to give what I consider the single most useful of advice for all humanity, it would be this: Expect trouble as an inevitable part of life, and when it comes hold your head high. Look it squarely in the eye, and say, 'I will be bigger than you. You cannot defeat me.'"

Ann Landers

Such wonderful advice from a woman who has been giving solutions to people's problems for decades.

I especially like her last line about not being defeated. We are all different, but I felt defeated after my partner's untimely death. It wasn't fair. He suffered too much. It wasn't fair. I suffered too much. It wasn't fair. Guess what? Life is not fair.

However, we don't need to be defeated by what is not fair. We must stand tall and be bigger than the problem. I believe Ann Lander's wisdom is excellent for those of us dealing with grief troubles.

"You have to embrace getting older. Life is precious, and when you've lost a lot of people, you realize each day is a gift."

Meryl Streep

If you are reading this book, you have lost a special person or persons in your life. You already realize that life is precious especially after losing someone dear to you.

The lesson we all need to remember is that each day is precious just like Meryl stated. We only have this day and tomorrow is not guaranteed. So, we need to make each day count.

As a part of this thought is the ability to say no to friends. Yes, learning to say no is difficult, but we need to say no more often. Sometimes we need alone time or just don't feel like doing something. Obligations are huge weights on our shoulders. Learning to say no is more important than learning Algebra.

As I was writing this book, a friend called asking me out to lunch. I said I would pass as I was busy trying to finish this book. He completely understood. I had to remember my goals. The day had been a gift for me as I was getting great satisfaction working on this new book. If I had gone to lunch, I would have been behind on my schedule.

Make each day a gift for yourself. You won't be disappointed.

"Too often we underestimate the power of a touch, a smile, a kind word, a listening ear, an honest compliment, or the smallest act of caring, all of which have the potential to turn a life around."

Leo Buscaglia

Even though we are dealing with our grief, we can also be messengers of love and hope to others. I love this quotation.

I always try to compliment friends and strangers every day of the week. It can be simple remarks like, "Wow, that is a beautiful dress" or "where did you get that great looking shirt? "

Besides the obvious compliments about one's looks or dress, I also like to compliment people on their remarks or positions on issues. I say things like, "You were so articulate when you spoke about the climate change crisis "or "you really summed up that point well on politics."

Smiles work well. Sometimes it might be the only smile that a person gets all day long. Again, our hearts may be breaking, but others may have even worse heartaches than we do. Kindness is so important, and we can be carriers of kindness when we are hurting as we understand hurt and sorrow.

"Once you replace negative thoughts with positive ones, you will start having positive results."

Willie Nelson

After a death, it is a struggle to be positive. However, as time passes it is easier to practice Willie Nelson's quote.

I have found his quote to be quite true. I started practicing being positive and those thoughts usually produced positive results.

As an example, I inherited a small IRA from my partner. These legal documents are always written in legalese that no one on the planet can understand, but the members of the financial community that write them.

I dreaded calling the company and asking questions about how to fill out the forms. As the beneficiary, it should have been so simple, but it wasn't. However, I used Willie's idea and called the company. The man on the phone was most patient and kind to me. He even sent me a link to my computer to fill out the forms online. It does work.

It is easy to get discouraged when you are dealing with sorrow every day. Willie Nelson's quote has been helpful for me, and I hope his idea works for you, too.

"Something terrible can happen to you and yet, the day after this something terrible, the sun rises, and life goes on. And therefore, so must you."

Martin Short

This is a great lesson for all of us who are grieving. It speaks to the tragedies we have all experienced. I think of my own dear Mother dying from cancer. I think of my young brother dying of AIDS before there was a cure. I remember the dogs we had to put to sleep when they became too ill to continue to live. Of course, the worst memory is Steve dying.

I had to get up the next morning after his death as I had two dogs to feed. I had to let them outside. The list of morning chores and obligations continued to grow the morning after his passing.

Steve was highly intelligent. He specifically told me to live life to the fullest. He wanted me to thrive not just survive. Martin Short's advice is the same as my late partner's words.

Rose Kennedy once said, "It is not tears, but determination that makes pain bearable." We must be determined to live and enjoy life. It will never be the same, but it can still be rewarding and enjoyable.

"Seize the Moment. Think of all those women on the Titanic who waved off the dessert cart."

Erma Bombeck

This is a famous quote from Erma, but it makes a good point.

Erma told the story about her sister. She would call her sister up and ask her out to lunch. Erma's sister always had some excuse like the house needs cleaning or I need to catch up on ironing. A few years later, her sister became ill and died. They never did have lunch.

Many years ago, we lived in Portland. We invited our friends Beve and Mary Lou over to go swimming in our pool. They turned us down saying that they needed to mow their grass as it was too long. Five minutes after hanging up, Mary Lou called back and said, "We are coming over. We can cut the lawn any day, but who knows when we will see you again." They were examples of seizing the moment knowing that tomorrows are not guaranteed.

The deaths of our loved ones teach us a valuable lesson about living each day to the fullest and not procrastinating about people we want to see or places we want to visit. Seize the moment!

"Live the wonderful life that is in you. Be afraid of nothing."

Richard Halliburton

This quote is powerful and full of promise.

Richard Halliburton was a famous travel writer, adventurer, and author who was the first person to swim the length of the Panama Canal. He was born in 1900 and died in 1939. He was presumed drowned after trying to sail a Chinese junk from Hong Kong to San Francisco.

Richard wrote wonderful travel books full of theatrical stories of his travels around the world. His books were full of fascinating tales of the adventures and people he met while touring the world.

I submitted his quote as sometimes after experiencing sorrow, some folks decide that traveling is over, and we should stay home. Richard did not believe in living a sedentary life. As a matter of fact, he said he never wanted to die in bed. He wanted an exciting death. Sadly, he got his wish.

Remember Richard's quote. He is basically saying, "Live, live, live." It is an important reminder that even though our spouse, relative or friend has died, we need to continue to live life to the fullest.

"Forgiveness does not change the past, but it does enlarge the future."

Paul Lewis Boese

This is such an optimistic quote.

I was critical of myself while Steve was in the hospital. Before he was in the hospital, I felt I could have done more to help him at home. The truth of the matter is I could not have done much more for him at either place. It was out of my control.

As I have noted before, we are all human and we do the best we know how in these awful medical situations.

I interpret this quote as meaning we can have a joyful future if we forgive ourselves for any real or imagined faults during our loved one's illness.

The future of your life after your spouse or special person has passed is up to you and no one else. You can choose to be lonely and depressed or go out and enjoy life as best you can.

Life is short so you must decide how you will live the remainder of your years without your partner or special person. I vote for enlarging the future.

"Keep busy with your work and your life. You can't become a professional mourner. It doesn't help you or others. Replay the good times. Be grateful for the years you had."

Betty White

This is my favorite quote in the book. Betty White knocks it out of the ballpark with her wise words.

I like the idea of not being a professional mourner. I hate going out to people's homes and talking all about Steve. I must be careful to limit the amount of time I do that. People don't want to hear it all the time, but they still give me wiggle room as it has only been a short time.

Replaying the good times is another good point. We had almost fifty years together. I always took tons of pictures so there are photographs everywhere in our house. The wonderful trips and fun times make me smile.

I also try to be grateful for the almost five decades we had together, many people have not been that lucky.

Keeping busy with my projects of making inspirational cards, writing columns, and publishing an occasional book keep me occupied with something purposeful.

I also continue to be involved with the Osher Lifelong Learning Institute which is located at Cal State at the San Bernardino campus in Palm Desert, California.

I even made cards of Betty's quote and have them all over the house and in my car. Her words are priceless.

> **"When someone is in your heart, they're never truly gone. They can come back to you, even at unlikely times."**

Mitch Albom

My first teaching assignment was in Yakima, Washington. It was there that I met the wonderful Mary Barbara Lemke. We lived in a three-story apartment building with hallways. We had the last two apartments on the third floor. I was in 305 and she was in 306. We became instant friends when I moved into the building.

She was about 55 years old, and I was twenty-two. She was a single medical secretary, and I was a young teacher. We just hit it off. It is too long of a story for this book, but we became best friends for life. She was truly one of the wisest people I have ever met. After her doctor retired, she moved down here to California to be near her sister and brother-in-law.

Mary Barbara lived to be 102 years old. She was a great and positive influence in my life and Steve's. She loved us unconditionally. She has never left my heart. Mary Barbara taught me so many things.

The fascinating thing about Mary Barbara is that she never traveled and spent most of her time in Yakima, Washington and Fillmore, California where her sister lived. However, she was one of the wisest people I had ever met. Plus, she had a great sense of humor. Mary Barbara had a bit of a temper sometimes and would use the F-bomb which would always make us laugh. Mary still is with me today. I know she is in the universe watching over me. She was deeply religious, but never forced her views on anyone. Having said that, she said many rosaries for us over the years. Guess what? Problems were always solved after she did her rosaries for us.

She took all her costume jewelry and made a frame with a musical staff. Using her jewels she made the first five notes to the song, "It Was the Best Time," sung by Liza Minnelli many years ago. It still hangs in my bedroom today.

I can still hear her laugh and her voice after all these years. Mitch Albom is correct that when someone is in your heart, they're never really gone. Mary Barbara Lemke will be with me always.

Your loved one will be in your heart always. I hope you can remember their voice and laugh even after years have passed. It is a real comfort.

"Don't wait for things to get better. Life will always be complicated. Learn to be happy right now, otherwise you'll run out of time."

Positive Thoughts

This is great advice. Right now, you are grieving the loss of someone special in your life. The pain of your loss is real, and it hurts you badly. This makes sense as death causes such pain.

Having said that, you also need to balance your sorrow with some sort of happiness. No, it doesn't have to happen immediately, but think of activities or people who can bring joy back to your life after your loss.

I have used myself as an example throughout this book. As I have said several times, life without Steve seemed pointless. However, my wonderful friends brought joy and laughter into my life. Yes, they mourned him, too. Our history had always been parties and dinners with close friends. Those events always provided lots of jokes and laughter. I needed that after Steve died. I just couldn't sit here at home and obsess about his passing.

Perhaps you enjoy golfing, hiking, or swimming. Maybe you enjoy playing cards or participating in a book club. It doesn't matter your interest but go back to it soon. These kinds of activities help you heal. Life is short and you don't want to run out of time.

"Art is for healing ourselves, and everybody needs their own personal art to heal up their problems."

Linda Ronstadt

Linda has wise advice for us all. She now has Parkinson's disease which has left her unable to sing. However, she encourages people to find healing through the arts.

It could be playing a musical instrument such as the piano, trumpet, or saxophone. However, it might be simply listening to music on your own CD player or your computer. The old quote that music soothes the savage beast is true. The savage beast is really the issues that upset us. Music can calm us down.

Art of any kind can do the same thing. It could be oil or watercolor paintings. It could also be pencil drawings, pottery, or sculptures. Healing can come from art.

During this time of grief, perhaps you can find some solace in the arts to help you manage your grief. I know that Steve loved to hear me play the piano. I admit I haven't played it much in the last few years. I do plan to take it up again as I think it would be healing for me. Plus, in a strange way, I feel Steve would like me to be using the piano more.

Hopefully, art will give you some healing in the weeks and months ahead.

"I like living. I have sometimes been wildly, despairingly, acutely miserable, racked with sorrow, but through it all, I still know quite certainly that just to be alive is a grand thing."

Agatha Christie

The author of mystery stories connects thoughts that millions of people have felt through the years. Yes, when we are racked with sorrow and miserable, it is challenging to see light at the end of the proverbial tunnel.

However, like Agatha Christie says, "It is a grand thing to be alive." We must embrace that thought even though we are experiencing overwhelming sadness. Yes, it is tough, but life is for the living. We only live once, and we need to make the most of it.

I don't believe any of our loved ones that have passed on would want to see us sad and lonely the rest of our lives. Adopting Agatha Christie's quote is a positive step for healing. I believe it is one of the strongest quotes I have ever read about survival. I suggest reading this quote often to appreciate living life with energy and purpose.

"We only live once. We all have an expiration date, after that we will never come again. I am not saying that to make you sad. I am saying that so you can cherish each moment in your life and be grateful that you are here, and you are special."

Pablo

I find Pablo's quote like others I have in this book. He is saying that living each day fully is important. We are all on the same journey, but none of us knows how long our own individual trip will last.

I used to tell my students that the five worst words in the English language were, "I wish I would have." I still believe those five words are extremely sad. How many times have we said them?

One of the effects of the death of a loved one is a wake-up call about our own lives. When death comes so close to us, it shakes us up. Have we done what we wanted in our lives? Have we spoken words to our loved ones telling them how we feel about them?

The bottom line is to get going on fulfilling your own bucket list. The clock does not stop ticking. By pursuing your goals, it also helps you to heal and focus on living life in the present.

"It isn't as bad as you think. It will look better in the morning."

Colin Powell

General Powell had a distinguished career in American history. He was the Secretary of State under President George W. Bush's administration. As a commander during the Vietnam War, he returned home with a Purple Heart and Bronze Star. His experiences during the war were rough. He saw fighting, death, and destruction.

However, he was always an optimist about life. I used his quote to make all of us think that even though we have lost someone we loved dearly, things always do look better in the morning after a night of sleep.

Of course, we are sad, but each morning gets better. Perhaps this morning will bring new stories about your loved one or new memories. Maybe you will find a special note or picture that lifts your spirits. You never know what unexpected gifts may come your way.

"Laughter is the sun that drives winter from the human face."

Victor Hugo

Laughter is especially important to healing.

Sometimes I believe we think it is disrespectful to laugh or enjoy good times with friends after our loved one has passed.

There are no rules about grief. I believe that laughter is especially important. It does help us relax and heal.

Steve and I had so much fun through the years at various parties, family gatherings, trips, and dinners. What we did the most at these events was laugh. Sometimes we would laugh hysterically as many of our friends were so darn quick witted.

There will always be plenty of time to be sad, but please let some humor and laughter into your life. It is extremely healthy for your mind and body.

"Grief, I've learned, is really just love. It's all the love you want to give but cannot. Grief is just love with no place to go."

Jamie Anderson

I thought this was a good quote to end the book.

Grief has such a negative connotation, and I liked that Jamie transformed the word to mean love. It was a wonderful concept.

Changing our idea of grief to mean love makes sense. We are wanting to love our husband, wife, mom, dad, son, daughter, grandparent, or friend who died. Why not incorporate grief to mean love even though we are unable to give them love personally?

I find the whole concept very comforting and healing. I will never look at the word grief again without thinking about the word love.

My Recent Columns on Grief

The Desert Sun Newspaper

April 5, 2022

May 3, 2022

The Desert Sun

April 5, 2022

Death. It is not a subject any of us relish talking about daily. It is something that we all know is going to happen to us, but we go through our lives pretending that it will never happen. It only happens to other spouses, families, or friends.

My partner Steve died in February at Eisenhower Hospital. We just missed celebrating our 49th anniversary together in March. I cannot accurately describe the feelings of loss, sadness, and emptiness. It is beyond heartbreaking. I wasn't prepared for it to happen. I thought he would rally, get better and return home from the hospital. However, it didn't happen. I got a call late one night to say he had passed. I so wish I had been there to hold his hand.

We started every morning having our coffee and reading The Desert Sun. As we got older our conversations became longer and the companionship of being together was even more special. Now I am reading the paper alone with my cup of coffee. The dogs still lay under the table waiting for some treat, but obviously it is not the same. It is my new normal.

"The irony of grief is that the person you need to talk to about how you feel is the person that is no longer there." Unknown. This quote really nails how I feel. Those readers who have lost someone special know this quote is powerful and true.

I am writing this column not to get sympathy, but to remind valley couples both gay and straight that they need to have all their documents and plans available to each other for when the inevitable happens.

We had planned years ago making a trust and finding a cremation company. We paid the cremation company ahead of time. This is important as they will come and pick up your loved one and help you with some of the forms needed for a death certificate. Death certificates are extremely important as you can't do anything legally or financially without one.

Calling Social Security is imperative as your Social Security check can change. If there is a change, you will have to make an appointment with them in person to show them your marriage certificate. They want the real certificate not a photocopy.

Technology has changed our world. It is so important to know your spouse's passwords for their phone, computer, iPad, and any other technical device. Plus, know your husband/wife's pin numbers for their bank accounts.

All the above is overwhelming. It doesn't have to all be done in a week or a month. Go at your own pace as you are not only dealing with paperwork, but daily grief.

Stay engaged with others. We were blessed with many good friends. They have been nothing short of saints during this difficult time. Everyone has been so supportive. My suggestion is to welcome your friends and family to your home if they ask to come visit. Accept dinner invitations, lunches or even a cup of coffee from your neighbors and friends. Being around people has helped me immensely. There is no sense sitting home feeling depressed.

Your dogs will feel the loss. Our dogs are very protective of me and the house. If they don't know you, they won't let you inside. Give your pets extra care as they experience their own kind of grief.

Don't be shy about picking up the phone and asking if you can come over to talk to someone. The phone will stop ringing and the sympathy cards will stop arriving in the mail. People go on with their lives, but they are more than willing to help if you ask. Everyone grieves in their own way and time, but never be hesitant about asking for advice or wisdom during such a challenging time in your life.

Betty White said it best, "Keep busy with your work and your life. You can't become a professional mourner. It doesn't help you or others. Replay the good times. Be grateful for the years you had."

Ray Matlock Smythe

The Desert Sun

May 1, 2022

I have been submitting columns for The Desert Sun for over twenty years. Last month I wrote a column titled, "After a loved one's death, how to go on and welcome help." I was not prepared for the reaction to that column. I received more e-mails from that one column that any other column I had written in two decades. The outpouring of readers sharing their stories of grief was heartbreaking. Sadder still was the fact that many of the people were still struggling with grief and had few people to help them with their sorrow. It demonstrated to me that many people are still trying to find comfort and acceptance about the loss of their loved one.

Here are a few more thoughts I would like to add to the column I wrote last month. I hope it will help people who are still coping with the loss of their spouse, child, relative or friend.

Don't go down the rabbit hole called should. Many people including myself asked questions like, "Should I have said this or done that? Should I have stayed longer at the hospital? Should I have guilt about this or that? "It is not healthy to do this kind of questioning.

There was a wonderful older doctor at Eisenhower Medical Center who took me out into the hall when my partner

Steve was losing his battle for life. He put his hand on my shoulder and said, "I absolve you of all guilt. You have done the best you can. You need to take care of yourself, or you will be no good to anyone." This compassionate doctor was brutally right. He told me people get Caregiver Syndrome which basically means they burn out trying to multitask everything and then get sick themselves. His kind advice was so welcoming as this was all new territory for me as it is for any of us.

After Steve passed, I was in a state of shock and denial. How could this be true? It was all so surreal. I didn't have a lot of time to grieve because I was trying to take care of our two dogs, run a house and do all the legal paperwork involved in my spouse dying. What I had were grief ambushes. They would sneak up on me at the oddest times. Four days after Steve died, I went to the grocery store to buy groceries. As I was pushing the cart down the aisle, I suddenly realized I was only buying food for me, not us. I could not get out of the store fast enough before dissolving into tears. I only share this story to prepare you for those little triggers that catch you off guard. It is ok that it happens. My 102-year-old friend Mary used to say that a good five-minute cry is cathartic. I agree.

Talk to other friends or family members that have lost a special person. I personally have sought out eight friends who have lost their spouses. I had them over for drinks or coffee. We sat at our dining room table and talked about how they coped. Often there were tears, but also laughter about sharing funny stories of our lives. Comparing coping strategies was invaluable for me. Talking to others who have experienced the same loss has been the BEST strategy for me to learn acceptance.

Acceptance. This is the toughest issue to deal with for most of us. Trying to wrap my head around not seeing my partner again is so difficult. People cope and grieve in different ways. One woman wrote me that she talks to her spouse every day. She doesn't know if he hears her or not, but it makes her feel good. Some people shared that they write in a journal each day telling their loved one their feelings or even how their day went. I try my best to follow Betty White's ideas of replaying the good times and being grateful for the years we had.

I also walk every day with my neighbors. Walking is very cathartic for me. You see the beauty of our mountains, the gorgeous flowers, and stunning landscapes of our desert. Nature to me has always been very healing. It is hard to be depressed when you are getting some exercise and surrounded by Nature's wonders.

Google quotes about grief and sorrow. Yes, I have found these to be great. I even make cards of the quotes and post them on my refrigerator, computer, and desk. I even taped one quote on my car dashboard. It keeps you focused on dealing constructively with your grief.

Let me share several that I felt were most helpful to me.

"Death ends a life, not a relationship." Mitch Albom

"Little by little, grief slowly fades. But love always burns brightly."

"Activity and Sadness are incompatible." Unknown

I hope that these suggestions will help bring comfort to readers who are going through the grief process. May these ideas bring you some acceptance, healing, peace, and serenity.

Ray Matlock Smythe

Steve Edward Oliver

Steve Edward Oliver passed away peacefully on February 23, 2022, at Eisenhower Medical Center in Rancho Mirage, CA. He died from complications from Lupus.

Steve was born on August 21, 1949, in Portland, Oregon. His parents were Mack and Marilyn Oliver. He attended Jefferson High School. He enrolled in Portland State University where he earned a Bachelor of Science degree. Then he became a student at Western States Chiropractic College where he earned his Doctor of Chiropractic degree in 1975.

Steve loved being a chiropractic physician. It was the supreme joy and passion of his life. He not only had a private practice, but also was the Academic Dean of the college, Vice-President of the college and a teacher of chiropractic techniques. He loved teaching students how to adjust patients. Every year he would receive outstanding evaluations from his students.

He was respected by everyone who knew him. Dr. Oliver was named the Chiropractor of the Year for the State of Oregon when he was only 29. He received many honors through the years. The last one was being named Professor

Emeritus by the University of Western States in June of 2012. He was truly an outstanding doctor who healed so many people through the years.

Steve moved with his partner Ray to Palm Springs 22 years ago. He started a chiropractic practice in Palm Springs, but it was short lived. He came down with Lupus about two years after arriving in the desert. As a result of the Lupus, he had to retire. This was the tragedy of his life having to give up his career. Although he was unable to continue treating patients, he volunteered in other programs.

Dr. Oliver was a generous and kind person. He volunteered for the AIDS Assistance Program for many years and was honored at the Evening Under the Stars event as their Volunteer of the Year. He was also active in the Osher Lifelong Learning Institute at the Cal State campus in Palm Desert. He not only took classes but was a donor to the program each year. As a matter of fact, he gave to many charities throughout his retirement years. He never mentioned his generosity, but he was always helping others with a check in the mail.

One of the other passions in his life were dogs. He loved his four-legged friends and always had one or two of them sleeping on his bed each night.

Steve was a role model for fighting the disease of Lupus. He was in pain 24/7, but he didn't complain. He suffered a great deal at the end of his life, but he never gave up. Steve made the planet a better place when he was alive by helping so many people with their pain and giving to others on many different levels.

He is survived by his partner of 48 years Ray Smythe, his brother Dave Oliver and his wife Julie, his older brother Kent Oliver, his nephew Michael and his wife Cristina, Dwayne Oliver and his wife Jenn, John Oliver, Matthew Oliver and his wife Chandra and his niece Erica and her husband Joe Olbinski. Plus, many friends here in the desert and in Portland.

We would also like to thank the nurses, doctors and technicians at Eisenhower Medical Center who worked so valiantly to save his life.

Author Biography

Ray Matlock Smythe received a Bachelor of Arts degree in Education from Western Washington University in Bellingham, Washington. Part of his sophomore year was spent in London, England as an exchange student at the City Literary Institute. He received his Master of Arts degree in Teaching from Lewis and Clark College in Portland, Oregon. Mr. Smythe taught American history for 39 years in middle and high school in Washington, Oregon, and California.

He has earned many accolades during his career. The four awards that were most meaningful to him were: being named the 1985 finalist for the Oregon State Teacher of the Year, being chosen as the 1987 Portland Trailblazers Educator of the year, being honored as the 2000-2001 Teacher of the Year at David Douglas High School and having the Marywood Palm Valley School Yearbook dedicated to him the year he retired.

This is Ray's 7th book. You may go to Amazon.com to view previously published books by Mr. Smythe.

Mr. Smythe may be reached at Rayme49@aol.com.

Made in the USA
Monee, IL
19 August 2022

11107867R00056